Cat Magick

WEEKLY PLANNER

ROCK
POINT

A Magickal Beginning

Every cat is magickal, not just those that house a familiar spirit.
They are disguised as little balls of fur, but in reality,
they have some pretty spectacular superpowers.

Hello there. Welcome to the magickal world of the cat. If this book has found its way to you, there may be a feline familiar that is working on your behalf. Or perhaps you have been curious about what kind of magick a cat can bring into your life. If you already work with feline energy, then maybe you're looking to dive a little bit deeper. Or even, you already practice other magickal workings in your life and are seeking to add a new one.

A cat's connection to the spirit world is virtually unparalleled, acting as a messenger and guide for their humans. The auric field and vibrational frequency of cats helps us connect to the realm of Spirit on a deeper level. When a familiar spirit chooses a witch and manifests in the physical form of a cat, their magickal power is unrivaled by any other animal. They teach us, lend us power and magick, deliver messages, stand as a guardian and protector, and come to our aid for spiritual growth and healing.

Whether you currently have a cat, have been thinking about adopting one, or would simply like to learn how to work with the mysterious and magickal energies that felines can bring into your life, you will find that spread across this weekly planner. Yes, you can still invoke and work with cat energy even if you do not or cannot have one in your life. These furry and often mischievous little creatures choose to work alongside us as long as we allow them into our lives.

Within these pages, you will learn some of the history of cat worship. You will learn invocations to call feline deities and spirits so that you can begin to work with them and their energies. You will gain knowledge regarding the different energies of animal messengers and guides, how and why they come into your life, and how to incorporate their power into your rituals and spell work.

By the end, you will leave with a deeper understanding of what it means to have a true familiar and how to work with them in your magickal practice. With spells and workings included to help you on your journey, discover how to work with cats instinctually, allowing them to assist and guide you. I have learned that as a magickal being, we should feel compelled to show up and listen to what needs to be heard or tended to. More often than not, cat energy tells us that we need to show up for ourselves in ways that we haven't before.

Are you ready to commune with Spirit? If so, let's get started.

Egyptian Goddesses

The most widely known of the Egyptian cat deities is Bast or Bastet, the sister of Sekhmet. Sekhmet is a cat goddess of ancient Egypt, depicted as a lioness and a warrior goddess. She was seen as the protector of the pharaohs as she led them into battle.

Bast appeared from the second dynasty in or around the mid-thirtieth century BCE. Ruins of the goddess's temple still stand in the city of Bubastis, where annual festivals were held to honor her. She was the goddess of fertility, pregnancy, and childbirth. She was also the goddess of cats themselves and a known protector.

Because of her connection to the sun god, she was viewed as a solar deity; however, she was often called the "eye of the moon." While her original form shows her as another lioness goddess, she later took on the form of a smaller cat. The domestic cat is seen as a living incarnation of the goddess. Bast protects the home, women, and children, and ensures that the mice and rats stay away.

♦ Invocation of the Goddess Bast ♦

If you feel called to work with Bast, you can create an altar for her with images of cats and/or lions. Offerings of raw meat, milk, or honey are appropriate. Use this invocation to the goddess to call upon her and her energies:

> *Cat goddess from the Nile*
> *Come sit with me for a while*
> *Honored protector Bast*
> *Power and wisdom vast*
> *This I ask of you*
> *Through this working I do*
> *Goddess, Eye of the Moon*
> *Help me with this boon.*

SEKHMET AND THE SUN

While Mafdet, the first known feline deity in ancient Egypt, was the protector of the Sun god Ra—from harm during his daily voyage across the sky—Sekhmet was known as a wild goddess who would fulfill the vengeful power of the god Ra. She was known as the Eye of Ra. Many historical texts suggest that she would breathe fire and that the hot winds of the desert were the result of her breath.

As a warrior goddess, if one should fall in battle, the goddess would continue to protect their spirit and see them into the afterlife. While some believe she caused plagues to serve as messengers for Ra's vengeful spirit, she was also known as a healing goddess and was called upon to ward off illness and disease.

Sekhmet and Bast, her sister, became known as two aspects of the same goddess. While Bast took on the image of a smaller cat of a gentler nature, Sekhmet kept the lioness aspect.

As known protectors of the Sun god Ra, the Sun holds its own powerful energies, and we can use specific timing throughout the day to aid our spell and ritual work. You can also connect with solar feline energies such as the lion or Sekhmet to help facilitate Sun magic into your workings.

- **Sunrise/Dawn:** New beginnings, manifestation, hope, charging energies
- **Morning:** Growth, building, relationships, wealth
- **Noon:** Protection, justice, health, courage, success
- **Afternoon:** Clarity, resolution, business communication
- **Sunset:** Endings, release/letting go, banishment, divination

WEDNESDAY	THURSDAY	FRIDAY	SATURDAY

FELINE BLESSINGS

We already mentioned Mafdet, Sekhmet, and Bast. All three deities had their own cat form, making the Egyptians a people who worshipped cats or associated felines with deity. This is also true for other cultures.

In India, she is Shashti, the goddess of reproduction and vegetation.

In China, she is known as Li Shou, part of the Chinese creation myth that says in the beginning cats were appointed by the gods to oversee everything.

The ancient Polish people worshipped the spirit Ovinnik, which would often come in the guise of a black cat.

In Greek mythology, the goddess Hecate shape-shifted into a cat to escape the monster Typhon, and then became the protector of all cats.

The Welsh goddess Cerridwen had white cats that carried out her orders on Earth.

It is not strange, then, that many folklore stories attribute luck and good fortune to cats. A custom of Renaissance-era Great Britain was for house guests to kiss the family cat upon arrival. In rural Italy, hearing a cat's sneeze blessed you with good fortune. In southern Scotland, a strange black cat on your porch would bring the dweller good fortune. These ancient cultures knew that felines were magical creatures and were meant to be treasured.

♣ Lucky Cat Invocation ♣

Should you need a bit of luck yourself, call upon the mystical good fortune of the cat! Use the following invocation to call upon their lucky energy:

> *Cat of Luck and Cat of Fortune*
> *Bring to me my fair portion*
> *Please let the money flow*
> *As I watch the wealth grow*
> *Good luck is on the way*
> *Holding true each and every day*
> *With harm to none*
> *As I ask, it shall be done.*

MONDAY

....

TUESDAY

....

WEDNESDAY

....

THURSDAY

....

FRIDAY

....

SATURDAY

....

SUNDAY

....

MONDAY

TUESDAY

WEDNESDAY

THURSDAY

FRIDAY

SATURDAY

SUNDAY

The Great Sphinx in the Al Giza Desert is possibly one of the greatest tributes to the feline.

MONDAY

TUESDAY

WEDNESDAY

THURSDAY

FRIDAY

SATURDAY

SUNDAY

The Quechua Indians of South America made offerings to the cat spirit, Coca, to prevent temperamental flare-ups that could call down lightning.

MONDAY

TUESDAY

WEDNESDAY

THURSDAY

FRIDAY

SATURDAY

SUNDAY

In the ancient Mexican civilizations of the Olmecs, Mayans, and Aztecs, the jaguar was worshipped as a deity.

The Goddess Freya

The Norse people worshipped the goddess Freya. She was the goddess of love, beauty, domesticity, and womanhood.

As Freya is the goddess of love, she embraces a sexual love, and she shares it willingly—even trading sex with four dwarfs for her most favored piece of jewelry, a beautiful amber necklace. In fact, her sexual favors gave her bargaining power. She was a woman who knew what she wanted and was not afraid to go after it. Her mastery of magick, which she taught freely, included the ability to influence the fate and fortunes of others, for which she was enormously respected. Her independent spirit helped her carve her own path.

She, like cats, was also a dramatic set of opposites. Freya was vicious and cunning, yet soft and sweet. As a war goddess, the thunder god, Thor, gifted her the cats that pulled her chariot. Male cats, their masculine energy created a balance with her feminine energies.

♣ Invocation of Freya's Battle Cats ♣

It takes great courage to run into battle, especially when you feel smaller than the enemy, as Bygul and Trjegul may have. If you feel you need a little extra courage, call on these two battle cats for help.

Hail! Freya's cats of battle!
For this obstacle I shall tackle
Brave and fierce I need to be
I ask that you come to me
Strength and courage you bring
A victory cry I will sing!

Ritual for Action and Courage with Bygul and Trjegul

Use this ritual when you need to be spurred into action and lack the courage to do so.

YOU WILL NEED

- A red taper candle
- Cauldron or fireproof dish
- Lighter or matches
- Clear alcohol (Everclear burns cleanest)
- 1 teaspoon dried thyme
- 1 teaspoon dried basil
- Incense of your choice
- Small glass vial with stopper

DIRECTIONS

1. Go into your sacred space.
2. Place the red candle and the cauldron or fireproof dish on your altar.
3. Cast a circle.
4. Light the red candle, then say the Invocation of Freya's Battle Cats (see previous page). (**Note**: Be careful when working with fire, taking the necessary precautions.)
5. Pour a small amount (about 1 teaspoon) of the alcohol into the cauldron.
6. Sprinkle in the dried thyme and basil.
7. Using the red candle, light the ingredients in the cauldron. (Please remember to be careful when working with fire and especially with the alcohol flame.)
8. Recite the Invocation of Freya's Battle Cats two more times.
9. Let the fire in the cauldron burn out completely.
10. Light the incense and use smoke to cleanse the glass vial.
11. Once the ash in the cauldron has cooled, collect the ash, place it in the glass vial, and replace the stopper.
12. Use the red candle to drip wax onto the vial stopper to seal it.
13. Snuff out the red candle.
14. Bid farewell to Bygul and Trjegul.
15. Open the circle. (**Note**: Make sure all fire is out.)

NOTES	SUNDAY	MONDAY	TUESDAY

WEDNESDAY	THURSDAY	FRIDAY	SATURDAY

MAGICKAL DAYS OF THE WEEK

Each day of the week holds a specific energy. When we align cat magick with the day that corresponds with what we are trying to achieve, it reinforces the intentions of the spell and adds power.

Sunday, the Sun's Day: Divine Masculine, success, happiness, joy, vitality, creativity, confidence

Monday, the Moon's Day: Dreams, the subconscious, intuition, scrying, divination, water magick, emotion, women's magick, domestic issues

Tuesday, Mars's Day: Quick action, ambition, sexual potency, passion, personal strength, self-assertion, victory, protection

Wednesday, Mercury's Day: Communication, technology, focus and alertness, learning, writing

Thursday, Jupiter's Day: Luck, abundance and prosperity, increasing and preserving wealth, business

Friday, Venus's Day: Divine Feminine, love, relationships and friendships, beauty, glamour magick, peace and harmony

Saturday, Saturn's Day: Protection, banishing and binding, communing with ancestors and departed spirits, overcoming obstacles

Once you become familiar with aligning your magickal intentions to a given day, the more you learn, the more you'll be able to combine into your workings, and the stronger your rituals will become.

MONDAY

....

TUESDAY

....

WEDNESDAY

....

THURSDAY

....

FRIDAY

....

SATURDAY

....

SUNDAY

....

MONDAY

TUESDAY

WEDNESDAY

THURSDAY

FRIDAY

SATURDAY

SUNDAY

An old sailors' tale warned against harming the ship's cat, which would guarantee stormy seas, drownings, and even sinking.

MONDAY

TUESDAY

WEDNESDAY

THURSDAY

FRIDAY

SATURDAY

SUNDAY

In France and Wales, there was a legend that if a girl stepped on the tail of a cat, she would have bad luck in love.

MONDAY

TUESDAY

WEDNESDAY

THURSDAY

FRIDAY

SATURDAY

SUNDAY

In colonial America, if a cat spent the day looking out the window, rain was coming. If they sat with their backs to the fire, a cold front was on the way.

Ritual to Embrace Your Wild Feminine

Use this ritual to get in touch with and honor the wild feminine that lives within you.

YOU WILL NEED

- A piece of cat-print clothing
- Outdoor space where you feel comfortable
- 3 pink candles
- 3 red candles
- 3 black candles
- Holders for all candles that will allow them to sit safely in an outdoor space
- 3 to 5 images that mean "wild feminine" to you
- Lighter or matches
- Music that makes you want to dance and feels a bit "wild" and a device to play it on, such as your phone
- Journal and pen

DIRECTIONS

1. Wear your cat-print piece of clothing.
2. Go into your outdoor space.
3. Set up the candles in a level area where there is no concern about them falling over. (Use extra caution when working with fire in an outdoor setting. Check any local fire bans.)
4. Place any images of the wild feminine in the space on the ground.
5. Cast a circle.
6. Say the Invocation of the Wild Feline Feminine (see next page).
7. Light the candles. (**Note**: Be careful when working with fire, taking the necessary precautions.)
8. Say the Invocation of the Wild Feline Feminine a second time.
9. Begin playing music.
10. Dance! Dance around the candles and the images.

11. Feel the energy of the wild feline feminine as it moves into this space and moves and flows around you and within you.

12. Dance until the song is done. You can repeat or play another if you feel called to do so.

13. Walk around the candles, gazing into the fire. Fire is passion.

14. Say the Invocation of the Wild Feline Feminine a third time.

15. View each image. What feelings do they evoke?

16. Sit for a moment and concentrate on your wilder nature, your passions, your inner fire, and the feelings that arise from the wild feminine images.

17. Make notes in your journal about how you are feeling.

18. Snuff out the candles.

19. Open the circle. (**Note**: Make sure all fire is out.)

20. Please remember to pick up after yourself if you venture out into a park or wild space. Leave-no-trace rules apply here!

❧ Invocation of the Wild Feline Feminine ❧

Calling upon the sacred wild feminine can empower you. When this wild energy comes from the feline, it can fill you with confidence, bolster your independence and reliance on yourself, and allow you to see and feel the divine within yourself.

Feline wild and feminine
Bring to me your passion
Free and true to self
With confident grace and stealth
This I ask of you
Goddess energy to imbue.

NOTES	SUNDAY	MONDAY	TUESDAY

CRYSTAL CORRESPONDENCES

Cats are a symbol of the wild feminine/Divine Feminine through their association with goddess energy. Similarly, crystals are powerful magickal allies. They boost our own energies and that of the spell. They protect, help heal, and facilitate communication between our higher selves, the Universe, Deity, and our guides. We can charge them for a specific purpose and carry them as a talisman or use them to create grids.

Crystals can be added to mojo or charm bags along with herbs and other magickal items for a variety of uses, including protection, sleep, money drawing, and healing. When we use all of our magickal knowledge and incorporate tools such as magickal timing, it takes less energy from ourselves to work the spell and requires less energy from our familiar. Use this wisdom to aid you and give you that needed boost without tapping into your own precious well of energy.

Healing: Amethyst, clear quartz, bloodstone, lepidolite, labradorite, agate, sugilite

Protection: Black obsidian, black tourmaline, smoky quartz, labradorite, jet

Communication: Sodalite, petalite, fluorite, blue lace agate

Love: Rose quartz, garnet, ruby, rhodochrosite, rhodonite

Money: Jade, pyrite, goldstone, emerald, citrine, tiger's eye

Divination: Selenite, moonstone, labradorite, petalite, lapis lazuli

Calming/sleep: Amethyst, selenite, moonstone, aquamarine, bloodstone

Fertility: Pink tourmaline, red/orange carnelian, moonstone, garnet, green aventurine

Happiness and joy: Citrine, sunstone, dalmatian jasper, tiger's eye

MONDAY

TUESDAY

WEDNESDAY

THURSDAY

FRIDAY

SATURDAY

SUNDAY

MONDAY

TUESDAY

WEDNESDAY

THURSDAY

FRIDAY

SATURDAY

SUNDAY

*Making an appearance in Macbeth is a gray
cat named Grimalkin, believed to have magickal
powers of predicting the future.*

MONDAY

TUESDAY

WEDNESDAY

THURSDAY

FRIDAY

SATURDAY

SUNDAY

*The dark, melanistic fur of the black cat is akin
to the dark feathers of the raven and the crow,
which were believed to be harbingers of death.*

MONDAY

TUESDAY

WEDNESDAY

THURSDAY

FRIDAY

SATURDAY

SUNDAY

Like Lilith, who refused to be domesticated and was forced into a life of subservience, the cat is unapologetically independent.

MONDAY

TUESDAY

WEDNESDAY

THURSDAY

FRIDAY

SATURDAY

SUNDAY

When a cat is stroked, the yielding electric sparks are believed to interfere with the spiritual or supernatural world.

Animal Familiars

An animal familiar is a spiritual being or entity that makes a pact with a witch to assist in their magickal workings, to lend support, power, and companionship. They can assume many forms, but animals are the most common.

If you are one of the fortunate who has a true familiar, you know that it is a bond like no other. It goes beyond that of a cherished pet and beyond the connection that you have with an animal guide. While familiars are also guides, it is important to remember that not all guides are familiars, just like a beloved pet, even a cat, may not be your familiar.

Familiars choose the individual they work with and can also choose their form. While witches report having a dog, rat, snake, or other reptile, or even a bird as a familiar, it would seem that the most common choice is the cat. It is believed that the energetic makeup of the feline is more accepting of the familiar spirit's magick and overall energy. It is also common to have a familiar spirit that will come back to you in another form—reincarnation, so to speak.

Having a familiar is a true gift. When that familiar comes in the form of a cat, it is a unique and extremely magickal experience. When you combine the natural energies of the feline with those of a familiar spirit, it is remarkable. They sit in the circle with us, lend us their power for ritual and spell work, serve as protectors and guardians, can act as an anchor in this realm when we travel in the astral world, and so much more.

Ritual to Reveal Your Feline Familiar to You

Perform this ritual if you want or need to find your familiar.

YOU WILL NEED

- A cat candle or a plain black candle
- Lighter or matches

TIP If you can find a cat candle, it might facilitate a quicker response or answer to this working. A cat candle can typically be found online or in local occult/metaphysical stores. Please note that the color of the cat candle is not important to this working. If you cannot find a cat candle, then I suggest using a black candle in its place, as this color is often associated with magick.

DIRECTIONS

1. Place the candle on your altar or in a personal sacred space.
2. Cast a circle.
3. Light the candle. (**Note:** Be careful when working with fire, taking the necessary precautions.)
4. Intone the following invocation three times:

> *If it's truly meant to be*
> *And you are to work with me*
> *Oh feline familiar spirit*
> *This is my call so hear it*
> *It is time for your reveal*
> *Let the magick be our seal.*
> *So mote it be (after the third time).*

5. Continue to watch the flame of the candle.
6. Take note if your cat enters the room or if you see one in your mind's eye.
7. If nothing shows up for you during this working, let the candle burn for another ten minutes, and then snuff it out. To continue the working, relight and burn for the next two nights (a total of three nights). Use the chant each time.
8. Open the circle. (**Note:** Make sure all fire is out.)

NOTES	SUNDAY	MONDAY	TUESDAY

WEDNESDAY	THURSDAY	FRIDAY	SATURDAY

TYPES OF MAGICKAL CATS

Animals are known messengers of Spirit and the gods. Cats are no exception. They can and will come into our lives when we need them to deliver those messages and help guide us. This can be as a visitor or messenger, a guide, or a familiar. What is the difference between the three and how can you distinguish whether a cat truly is your familiar? What roles do they truly play in our lives? How can we connect with them on an energetic level?

Messengers: An animal that comes to a person to specifically deliver a message from their higher self, the Universe, Spirit, their guides, their ancestors, or Deity. We do not seek these animals out; instead, they seek us out. Often, they come in corporeal form or in spirit form in a dream or through one's third eye. They may be there for a minute or even a few days depending on how long it takes you to acknowledge the message or if the message is of a more complex nature.

Guides: An animal that comes into one's life as a teacher, to offer guidance, support, protection, power, and wisdom, and to deliver messages. They have a personal relationship with the individual, although sometimes a person can have a guide even if they are not aware of it. Some people may have multiple guides—this is especially common among magickal people. They stay for long periods of time, sometimes for one's entire life.

Familiars: An animal that exists in the physical or metaphysical plane, but they can also choose to reincarnate and come back again and again, even returning in their witch's next life. Witches, shamans, and other magickal people have one, and they can only have one at any given time. Familiars can also take on the role of guide or messenger as well as cuddle with us in the evening.

MONDAY

TUESDAY

WEDNESDAY

THURSDAY

FRIDAY

SATURDAY

SUNDAY

MONDAY

TUESDAY

WEDNESDAY

THURSDAY

FRIDAY

SATURDAY

SUNDAY

If a cat suddenly shows up, or you find yourself dreaming about one, pay close attention because they are there to deliver a message.

MONDAY

TUESDAY

WEDNESDAY

THURSDAY

FRIDAY

SATURDAY

SUNDAY

Animal guides are referred to as spirit animals or totems in some cultures.

MONDAY

TUESDAY

WEDNESDAY

THURSDAY

FRIDAY

SATURDAY

SUNDAY

Some people describe the bond of a familiar to being similar to a soul mate connection. You sense their power, even as a kitten. You just know that they have chosen you.

Jaguars

The jaguar is the gatekeeper to the unknown and the mystical, and is a force of raw, primal energy. As an animal guide, they can show you how to access the Akashic records and even walk into your past lives. The Akashic records are a compilation of everything that has ever happened in the Universe, including thoughts, words, and emotions of every entity and life-form, not just humans, for the past, present, and future.

Jaguars can teach their charge how to reclaim their power by awakening that inner core energy. They are the embodiment of both the Moon and the Sun and, through that, are able to teach balance and show how to walk between and within liminal spaces.

Intense energy surrounds the jaguar and makes for a particularly powerful familiar. They are known for ruling the Underworld—considered the land without light in some cultures—and because of this, they gift their witch with the ability to pierce the veil of darkness and reach into it for power. Because they are mystical gatekeepers, they take on the role of showing the witch their path and purpose and guiding them along it. They embody lunar energy and aid in Moon magick as well as boost psychic abilities, intuition, and the ability to face the darkness head-on.

Reciting this will invoke the power and energies of the jaguar.
Burn one black and one gold candle.

Energies: Awakening/reclaiming inner power, guidance, intuition

Fierce hunter of the night
With strength and grace she strikes
Jaguar, gatekeeper to the unknown
Mystic realms and awakening the soul
She sees beyond the veil
And shows one to their true self.

Ritual to Reveal Your Feline Guide to You

Do this ritual to establish whether you have a feline guide or not.

YOU WILL NEED

- A cat candle or a plain black candle
- Lighter or matches

DIRECTIONS

1. Place the candle on your altar or in a personal sacred space.
2. Cast a circle.
3. Light the candle. (**Note:** Be careful when working with fire, taking the necessary precautions.)
4. Watch the flame of the candle. If using a cat candle, take note of how the light shifts over the shape of it as the flame flickers.
5. When ready, chant the following three times:

> *Feline guide*
> *If you're truly mine*
> *Make yourself known*
> *So our bond can grow.*

6. Continue to watch the flame of the candle.
7. Take note if your cat entered the room or if you see one in your mind's eye.
8. If nothing shows up for you during this working, let the candle burn for another ten minutes, then snuff it out. To continue the working, relight and burn the candle for the next two nights.
9. Open the circle. (**Note:** Make sure all fire is out.)

NOTES	SUNDAY	MONDAY	TUESDAY

WEDNESDAY	THURSDAY	FRIDAY	SATURDAY

LEOPARDS

Though the leopard and jaguar are the same as their melanistic counterparts, except for the genetic variance that colors them black, leopards do hold different energies. While they still carry that of the Divine Feminine, they bring different lessons with them.

There is a saying that "a leopard cannot change its spots," and while most apply this meaning in a negative connotation, this saying can also contain the leopard's most powerful guidance: to be unapologetically yourself. The leopard as an animal guide teaches us to trust our intuition and instincts and not to second-guess ourselves. The leopard shows their charge how to be self-reliant. As animals can often be found in the trees and have impeccable vision, they remind us that sometimes the answer to a problem is all about changing our perception.

As a familiar, the leopard lends a great deal of strength to their witch, always reminding them of who they truly are.

Reciting this will invoke the power and energies of the leopard.
Burn one black candle and one tan or light brown candle.

Energies: Confidence, divination, intuition

She wears her spots with pride
From her true self she never hides
Fierce power, free and untamed
Leopard huntress stalks the night
On the ground or from a tree
Changing perception to truly see
With patience she waits
Hidden in plain sight.

MONDAY

TUESDAY

WEDNESDAY

THURSDAY

FRIDAY

SATURDAY

SUNDAY

MONDAY

TUESDAY

WEDNESDAY

THURSDAY

FRIDAY

SATURDAY

SUNDAY

The black cats—melanistic leopards and jaguars—are commonly referred to as "black panthers."

MONDAY

....

TUESDAY

....

WEDNESDAY

....

THURSDAY

....

FRIDAY

SATURDAY

SUNDAY

Both the black jaguar and the black leopard come into your life as messengers, signaling that it is time to remove the mask that you are hiding behind.

MONDAY

TUESDAY

WEDNESDAY

THURSDAY

FRIDAY

SATURDAY

SUNDAY

Wear your spots with pride, as there is no need to hide them.

Ritual to Create a Fur Talisman

A talisman is an object imbued with magick through ritual or spell work that will grant protection from harm and can ward against negative or evil forces. It can also bring good luck.

To create a talisman, you must first decide what its purpose is. Once you know that, you can then collect or find the fur that you need. Don't be afraid to ask friends or family members for their cat's shed fur. If none of those cats' coloring corresponds to your need, then you might also be able to find it online. The next step is to figure out the container you would like to use for your talisman. Many people use lockets so that the talisman is worn without question in public settings. Small glass vials with stoppers are also a good choice.

YOU WILL NEED

- The container of your choice (locket or small glass vial with stopper)
- Incense
- Lighter or matches
- Shed cat fur in color that aligns with the talisman's purpose
- Candle, if using a glass vial, in the corresponding color to the spell work you are doing

DIRECTIONS

1. Cleanse the container of your choice with incense smoke by moving the vial through the smoke and then inserting the smoking end into the vial for a moment. Please use caution when using incense smoke.
2. Set the container and cat fur on your altar or in your sacred space.
3. Cast a circle.

4. Pick up the container and intone the following:

> *This [name the container—locket, vial, etc.] shall be for me*
> *A repository for this energy.*

5. Place the cat fur in the container as you intone the following:

> *The fur of the [name type of cat] I place in here*
> *To [name the working—heal, protect, bring good luck, etc.]*
> *A talisman I create*
> *Working for my aid.*
> *As I will, so mote it be.*

6. If you are using a glass vial, seal the stopper with candle wax. Using a corresponding color is recommended: black for protection, white for healing, etc. (**Note**: Be careful when working with fire, taking the necessary precautions.)
7. Open the circle. (**Note**: Make sure all fire is out.)

NOTES	SUNDAY	MONDAY	TUESDAY

WEDNESDAY	THURSDAY	FRIDAY	SATURDAY

CAT FUR COLORS

As witches, we know that everything is energy and those energies are different and varied depending on the object. The same can be true of cats. The following is a breakdown of domestic cat colors and the energetic powers they possess.

Black Cats: Protection and keeping negative entities and energies away. They are powerhouses when it comes to lending energy as a familiar.

Red/Orange/Yellow Cats: Vitality and corresponds to Sun and Mars energy. They might exude a more masculine energy because their coloring aligns with the Divine Masculine.

Blue Gray/Smoky Cats: Corresponds to the Divine Feminine and goddess energy. A shadow color, the cats hold the energy of balance, representing the "in between."

White Cats: Healing and purity. These cats have long symbolized spiritual enlightenment or rebirth.

Brown Cats: Earth energy. The fur can also be kept in a locket or vial to help you feel calm and grounded.

Color Point (Siamese) Cats: Luxury (wealth and prosperity), power, and wise leadership.

Persian Cats: Comfort, good luck, and good fortune. They have been known to be popular cats around businesses for this reason.

Calico (Tricolor) Cats: Represents the three aspects of the goddess—the maiden (white), the mother (red for blood), and the crone (black for wisdom and magick).

Two-Tone or Tuxedo Cats: Balance. These cats also carry a little bit of mischief, urging us to keep the work/play balance in our lives.

Tortoiseshell Cats: The Divine Feminine. They are highly clairvoyant and are protectors of children.

Tabby Cats: Change and transformation. These cats tend to be social and adventurous. They are keepers of the Universe's secrets and hold great wisdom.

MONDAY

TUESDAY

WEDNESDAY

THURSDAY

FRIDAY

SATURDAY

SUNDAY

MONDAY

TUESDAY

WEDNESDAY

THURSDAY

FRIDAY

SATURDAY

SUNDAY

*Use black fur in spells for cloaking and
shape-shifting.*

MONDAY

TUESDAY

WEDNESDAY

THURSDAY

FRIDAY

SATURDAY

SUNDAY

White fur can be used for gaining access to your Akashic records to promote spiritual and soul growth.

MONDAY

TUESDAY

WEDNESDAY

THURSDAY

FRIDAY

SATURDAY

SUNDAY

Tortoiseshell fur can help if you are in need of independence, especially in toxic relationships.

MONDAY

TUESDAY

WEDNESDAY

THURSDAY

FRIDAY

SATURDAY

SUNDAY

Use tabby cat fur for workings to help you "come out of your shell," for fortitude in social situations.

Masculine Lion Energy

The masculine energy of the big cats is held within the regal lion. Looking at images of him, it is easy to see why he is called the "King of Beasts." Some believe that the masculine energies of the lion serve as a protector from unwanted visitors to our planet. His mighty roar reverberates through the layers of the Earth, sending out the signal to stay away.

He symbolizes majesty, grace, leadership, strength, and courage. His vibrant yellow-gold mane is a symbol of solar energy in many ancient cultures, thus tying the lion to the Divine Masculine and the power of the Sun. Lion energy is one of warmth and vitality, drawing you in and infusing you with passion and a love of life.

If the mighty lion comes roaring into your life as a messenger, know that it is time to act. He often delivers messages that relate to standing in your power or taking your power back, stepping into a leadership role, calling in familial protection, or banishing fear to gain the courage to do what needs to be done. He may also be letting you know that you need to balance or tap into the Divine Masculine within you.

When the lion is your personal animal guide, he infuses you with the energy of the leadership role. People with lion guides are those who lead with seemingly effortless grace; they are naturals when it comes to taking the helm. He walks beside his charge, helping them maintain a balance within the ranks through strong ideals and morals while taking challenges head-on. He will guide them to ways of self-expression that are humble yet steadfast.

Ritual to Sync with Solar Energies

The following spell will help you align with the energy of the Sun and the lion. This spell should be worked during the day. If possible, be in an area where the Sun is shining brightly into the room.

YOU WILL NEED

- A small gold candle
- Your cat
- Lighter or matches

DIRECTIONS

1. Go into your sacred space.
2. Place the gold candle on your altar.
3. Cast a circle.
4. Bring the image of a warm summer day into your mind. Visualize the Sun shining brightly and feel its warmth upon your skin.
5. Ask your cat to help you harness the energy of the lion and the Sun; notice the characteristics that are the same between the cat and a lion. Do not be alarmed if the cat morphs into an image of a lion at this point. They are doing what you have asked and are bringing in that leonine vibration.
6. Light the gold candle. (**Note:** Be careful when working with fire, taking the necessary precautions.)
7. Bring your hands up on either side of the candle so you can feel its warmth but not get burned.
8. Continue to gaze upon the gold candle and its flame.
9. Once you feel the Sun/lion energy present, drop your hands and let the candle burn out.
10. Thank the Sun god, the Divine Masculine, the lion, and your cat for being there and for their assistance.
11. Open the circle. (**Note:** Make sure all fire is out.)

WEDNESDAY	THURSDAY	FRIDAY	SATURDAY

WORKING WITH THE LION

Those who encounter the lion as their familiar will find that he lends almost limitless power to their magickal workings. He also gives his witch the ability to soak up major solar energy and be able to channel it into their spells. "Lion people" often love summer and find themselves drawn to solar or fire deities and energies. Their lion familiar will teach them how to work with those energies with respect and how to honor their own Divine Masculine power, as we all hold this energy within us.

Witches and other magickal people who are graced with a lion familiar may find themselves as the leader of a coven or even a teacher of witchcraft, shamanism, or other spiritual paths. Lions have a close and intuitive alignment with their throat and crown chakras, naturally connecting them to higher universal energies and communication.

Reciting this will invoke the power and energies of the lion.
Burn a yellow or gold candle.

Energies: Divine Masculine energies, Sun magick, protection

> *Do not be fooled*
> *By his napping in the Sun*
> *Beneath the golden coat*
> *And mane untamed*
> *A fierce protector*
> *Lies in wait*
> *Strength and courage unrivaled*
> *Guardian of the pride*
> *Walking in confidence*
> *Hearing the lion's roar*
> *Come what may.*

MONDAY

....

TUESDAY

....

WEDNESDAY

....

THURSDAY

....

FRIDAY

....

SATURDAY

....

SUNDAY

....

MONDAY

TUESDAY

WEDNESDAY

THURSDAY

FRIDAY

SATURDAY

SUNDAY

Even though the bond with one's familiar involves taking care of them, the bond is really forged and strengthened through magickal workings.

MONDAY

TUESDAY

WEDNESDAY

THURSDAY

FRIDAY

SATURDAY

SUNDAY

Bond with familiar spirits in the form of stray cats by leaving out food and water, making a small shelter with a blanket, or talking to them when they are around.

MONDAY

TUESDAY

WEDNESDAY

THURSDAY

FRIDAY

SATURDAY

SUNDAY

Make a trip to a big cat sanctuary or a local zoo and you might encounter a lion or tiger coming up to the glass of their enclosure and staring intently at a person.

Metaphysical Beings

While other animals have the ability to see and feel energies, they do not compare to the cat. Many people say that cats are more discerning than dogs when it comes to giving their affection. This could be because cats can see and sense auras. They may choose to not interact closely when the aura is mucky. The exception to this is with their chosen human(s) as they will watch the auras or energy fields of those within the home.

Because a cat's energy, aura, and overall vibration align with the metaphysical world, it is no wonder that they are naturally drawn to spiritual people. Witches, shamans, and other magickal humans also have a frequency that opens them up to higher energies and realms.

Those who work magick and/or have spiritual practices tend to keep their energetic field "neater and cleaner" than those who do not. This is one of the reasons why cats are drawn to them. With spiritual people, cats simply have an easier time because they do not have to constantly clear the energetic field or raise their vibration. They can simply be, and that is a beautiful thing to them.

❧ Spell to See Energy or Auras ❧

Use this spell if you want or need to see different energies or auras.
Use a dark blue or an indigo candle.

Feline familiar, lend me your eyes
To look beyond the guise
The second sight please give to me
So that I may truly see
True vision is found
Now energies and auras abound.
So mote it be.

⚬ Ritual to Open the Crown Chakra ⚬

Use this ritual to open up your crown chakra to help you receive messages.

YOU WILL NEED

- A purple candle
- A carrier oil of your choice to dress the candle
- Dried mugwort
- Dried clary sage
- Lighter or matches
- A timer (you can use your phone)
- Pen and notebook or journal

DIRECTIONS

1. Go into your sacred space.
2. Rub the candle with the carrier oil and then roll it in the dried herbs.
3. Place the candle on your altar.
4. Cast a circle.
5. Light the candle. (**Note**: Be careful when working with fire, taking the necessary precautions.)
6. Intone the following three times:

> *Messages coming to me*
> *Help me so that I can see*
> *Delivered by feline familiar*
> *Help me so that I can hear*
> *From the Divine, Universe, and Spirit*
> *Help me so that I am open to it.*
> *As I will, so mote it be (after the third time).*

7. Set the timer for nine minutes.
8. Soften your gaze, or close your eyes if you feel comfortable, and clear your mind.
9. When the timer is done, write down any messages that may have come through in your notebook or journal.
10. Let the candle burn out completely.
11. Open the circle. (**Note**: Make sure all fire is out.)

NOTES	SUNDAY	MONDAY	TUESDAY

WEDNESDAY	THURSDAY	FRIDAY	SATURDAY

AURAS

Auras are invisible energy fields that surround everything and everyone and are part of a more complex system called the subtle energy body. If a cat's human's aura has been affected negatively, they will often come to them seemingly seeking attention, but in reality, they are trying to help them cleanse heavy energies. They may curl up in your lap or sit on your chest to clear the aura, often purring.

If the cat hisses at someone, take note. When they sense or see something in the aura of an unknown person that poses an energetic threat to them, they will typically hide. They are aware that something is going on with this person that makes them uncomfortable. This is a warning and likely an energy that you are not sensing yourself.

There are seven layers to the human aura, each connected to our overall health. Auras can be different colors, and each color is associated with its own meaning. Below is a quick list of some of the main aura colors and their meanings. Please note that auras are a much more complex subject of magickal work; below is just a simple guide to get you started.

Red: Well grounded, passionate, strong-minded

Orange: Adventurous, active, considerate

Yellow: Positive, creative, open-minded

Green: Kind, compassionate, communicator

Blue: Intuitive, peaceful, spiritual

Indigo: Sensitive, curious, inner knowing

Violet: Inquisitive, intelligent, connected to the spirit world

MONDAY

TUESDAY

WEDNESDAY

THURSDAY

FRIDAY

SATURDAY

SUNDAY

MONDAY

TUESDAY

WEDNESDAY

THURSDAY

FRIDAY

SATURDAY

SUNDAY

Never make your cat interact with anyone if they choose not to; there is a reason why they are leery of them.

MONDAY

. . . .

TUESDAY

. . . .

WEDNESDAY

. . . .

THURSDAY

. . . .

FRIDAY

SATURDAY

SUNDAY

The frequency or vibration of cats is one that naturally repels and transmutes negative energies.

MONDAY

TUESDAY

WEDNESDAY

THURSDAY

FRIDAY

SATURDAY

SUNDAY

A cat's purr is also an effective tool when it comes to cleansing an area.

Melanistic Big Cats

We've talked about the black cats already. They hold feminine energies and are said to be spiritual leaders that help us humans raise our vibrations. Instead of focusing on the leopard and jaguar, which are commonly called "black panthers," here we'll talk about the true black panther, who delivers the messages that it is time to face the darkness and the need for shadow work.

If the black panther is your animal guide, you will more than likely have an affinity for lunar energy and workings that revolve around the phases of the Moon. "Black panther people" typically love their alone time and tend to be night owls. As a guide, the black panther will teach their person to develop their natural psychic abilities. They can also help you unlock your sensual and sexual self.

Much like the black panther as a guide, a black panther familiar brings their witch powerful lunar magick. Those with a black panther familiar tend to be solitary witches and like to work with lunar goddesses and often dark goddess energy. Black panther familiars teach their witches not to fear the darkness that lives within all of us and will help them fully integrate their shadow self.

Because the black panther is the ultimate shape-shifter and a master of disguise, as a familiar they will bring this knowledge to their witch so that they too can cloak themselves and have the ability to move between worlds unseen. They will help increase the witch's psychic abilities as well as aid in divination or scrying spells.

Ritual to Invoke Big Cat Energy

Use this general ritual to invoke the big cat energy that is required in that moment.

YOU WILL NEED

- Pen
- Notebook or journal

DIRECTIONS

1. Go within your sacred space.
2. Cast a circle.
3. Intone the following chant three times:

> *Fierce and bold*
> *With beauty untold*
> *Your strength this circle will hold*
> *Powerful and mighty*
> *Big cat energy*
> *I ask that you come to me.*
> *As I will, so mote it be (after the third time).*

4. Be aware of who shows up for you. Write down any messages or impressions. Let them know why you have called them and remember to ask for their permission if you would like to use their energy in spell work. If they consent, then proceed with the working.
5. Thank the cat that showed up for their assistance and bid them farewell.
6. Open the circle.

NOTES	SUNDAY	MONDAY	TUESDAY

WEDNESDAY	THURSDAY	FRIDAY	SATURDAY

BLACK PANTHERS

Big cats are powerful creatures that have been coming to the aid of witches, shamans, and other magickal people for millennia. Every time we work with their energy, the experience is profound and magickal. There are stories that have been relayed of shocking interactions with big cats in the wild, within wildlife sanctuaries, and even at zoos. With that said, if you are struggling to connect with big cat energy, have faith that the one that shows up will have what you require. Most importantly, remember to be open to their messages and teachings when given.

As witches, we have the ability to call energy to us. We can invoke the power of the lion when we need courage. Because of the high levels of melanin that cloak their spots, black panthers can help us work within the shadows and darkness. They can show you how to slip into the shadows to see into the beyond and how to boost your own psychic abilities. This power animal is an especially fierce ally for mothers who need help leaving a toxic environment or relationship.

We may work with just the energy of the animal or call the spirit of that animal to us. We can invite them into our magick circle to aid in spell work or ask them to walk with us when we need that extra guidance and support.

Reciting this will invoke the power and energies of the black panther. Burn a black candle.

Energies: Self-reliance, Moon magick, Divine Feminine energies

She moves silently through the night
Unseen, cloaked in darkness
Stalking the jungle with stealth
Presence revealed only when the time is right
Black panther, sacred Divine Feminine
And a force to be reckoned with.

MONDAY

TUESDAY

WEDNESDAY

THURSDAY

FRIDAY

SATURDAY

SUNDAY

MONDAY

TUESDAY

WEDNESDAY

TUESDAY

FRIDAY

SATURDAY

SUNDAY

In the Andean shamanic tradition, the Lower World (not to be confused with Christian hell) is where our animal guides reside.

MONDAY

TUESDAY

WEDNESDAY

THURSDAY

FRIDAY

SATURDAY

SUNDAY

Mother Nature tries to achieve balance, containing both the Divine Feminine and the Divine Masculine to come together in harmony.

MONDAY

TUESDAY

WEDNESDAY

THURSDAY

FRIDAY

SATURDAY

SUNDAY

*It is important to remember that each cat
is to be respected, regardless of their size.*

MONDAY

TUESDAY

WEDNESDAY

THURSDAY

FRIDAY

SATURDAY

SUNDAY

Even if higher magick is being worked along with complex spells or rituals, the cat will match it, power for power.

Nocturnal Beings

R emember that both cats and witches are associated with the night, a time shrouded in mystery and magick. The "witching hour" is between midnight and three in the morning. While some rituals are done during this time, most witches are getting their *zzzz*s. The witch's cat, however, is up and on the prowl.

The nocturnal nature of the feline naturally aligns them with the Moon. Moon energy is feminine and corresponds to the Divine Feminine. Just as Monday is the Moon's Day, the phases hold their own energies that we can draw and call on to strengthen our workings and intentions. Other sources we can use to call on the Moon include the color silver and the crystal moonstone.

Many witches work with Moon and goddess energies, so having a cat as a friend or familiar can strengthen the relationship with lunar energy and, through that, the Divine Feminine. A witch's cat can also aid in lunar and magickal workings. Moon energy can be associated with emotions, intuition, dreams, visions, illuminating what needs to be seen, releasing and cleansing, and, of course, the Divine Feminine.

❧ Moon Offerings ❧

Make a Moon offering when working with the energy of the Moon. There are many objects that can be cleansed in the moonlight, simply by setting them out overnight to bathe in the light. An offering you can make to the Moon in exchange for its energy is Moon water—water left under the moonlight during your chosen Moon phase, usually the Full Moon, to infuse it with Moon energy.

⌦ Ritual to Sync with Lunar Energies ⌦

Here is a simple spell to help you sync with the energy of the Moon and
the lunar vibration of your feline familiar. This spell should be worked
at night. If possible, be in an area where you can see the Moon.

YOU WILL NEED

- A small silver candle
- Lighter or matches
- Your cat

DIRECTIONS

1. Go into your sacred space.
2. Place the silver candle on your altar.
3. Cast a circle.
4. Bring the image of a full, glowing Moon into your mind. Visualize the
   moonbeams shining down.
5. Light the silver candle. (**Note:** Be careful when working with fire,
   taking the necessary precautions.)
6. Intone the following:

   > *Goddess of the Moon*
   > *Feline bathed in silver light*
   > *With your energy I attune*
   > *Give to me the sight*
   > *Intuition, visions, and dreams*
   > *Together we stalk the night*
   > *Through her magickal beams.*

7. Hold your cat for as long as they allow you to
   and focus on the silver candle.
8. Let the candle burn out.
9. Thank the Moon, goddess, Divine Feminine, and
   your cat for being there and for their assistance.
10. Open the circle. (**Note**: Make sure all fire is out.)

NOTES	SUNDAY	MONDAY	TUESDAY

⟡ CAT AND MOON MAGICK ⟡

While all felines, and most nocturnal predators, have eyes with a mirror-like structure behind their retinas to promote night vision, domesticated cats are the only feline that have vertical slit pupils. This optimizes their perception and vision in bright day light as well as dim night light.

The black cat's dark fur is a symbol of the night, a time when witches worked, danced naked under the Full Moon, brewed curses, and made sacrifices to their heathen gods, or this was what was believed by Christianity.

Both leopards and jaguars are big cats that are one with the night and lunar energy. Black panthers tend to be night owls as well.

When we align our spells with the different Moon phases, it will further empower them with the energy of that phase.

 New or Dark Moon: Setting intentions, manifesting, new beginnings, shadow work

 Waxing Crescent: Nurturing, self-love, compassion, courage, positive mind-set

 First Quarter: Drawing things to you such as a new job, love interest, success, money, etc.

 Waxing Gibbous: Fertility, endurance, breaking through what one may be resisting

 Full Moon: Release, letting go of what no longer serves us, cleansing, protection

 Waning Gibbous: Minor banishing, cleansing

 Last Quarter: Removing obstacles, allowing flow with ease, breaking addictions

 Waning Crescent: Major banishing, removing toxic relationships or situations

MONDAY

TUESDAY

WEDNESDAY

THURSDAY

FRIDAY

SATURDAY

SUNDAY

MONDAY

TUESDAY

WEDNESDAY

THURSDAY

FRIDAY

SATURDAY

SUNDAY

Back in the day, domestic cats hunted cobras and other venomous snakes; today they are still stealthy hunters, stalking the night.

MONDAY

TUESDAY

WEDNESDAY

THURSDAY

FRIDAY

SATURDAY

SUNDAY

It is advised to always cast a circle when working with a feline familiar because of the intense energy and higher levels of magick working alongside them.

MONDAY

TUESDAY

WEDNESDAY

THURSDAY

FRIDAY

SATURDAY

SUNDAY

Feline familiar spirits come and go as they choose, appearing every few days, syncing with Moon cycles, or coming when magick is afoot.

The Support of a Magickal Being

A familiar chooses a witch and comes into their physical form with the agreement that they are here to teach and guide, deliver messages, assist, protect, and lend power and magick to workings. A familiar can and will act as an energetic conduit for their witch. This is especially evident when magickal workings are being done. Once you and your familiar are bonded, you should be able to tell when the familiar is pouring their magick or energy into a spell.

The more that you work with your familiar, the more comfortable it will feel, and you will begin to notice more of the things they do without being asked. One of the benefits of a cat familiar is that they act as a buffer for the magick that is taking place. Even with a protective circle in place, you usually need to clear and cleanse a magickal space after a working. With a feline familiar, you will find that the need to clear and cleanse becomes less and less necessary. They automatically keep the energy flowing throughout a ritual or spell and then help clear it out afterward, ensuring that any residue is taken care of.

Cats take protecting their territory seriously, so they also do a wonderful job of keeping dark entities or negative spirits away from the house. The auric field of a cat is naturally repelling toward unsavory spiritual guests. If something does make its way in, your familiar will let you know and then help you deal with it. They will guide you as to how to go about it and then lend you the power and magick required.

Because your feline familiar is a fierce protector, you can ask for assistance when it comes to securing the wards (magickal defense system) around the home. Your feline familiar will provide power and magick to reinforce what is already in place and also show how it can be even stronger.

Ritual to Call Your Familiar's Energy into the Circle

Use this ritual to call your familiar's energy into the circle to assist with and enhance your spell work. This spell may change your cat's mind about their participation but does not affect their free will. Remember that the familiar spirit can be called separately without any harm to the cat that serves as their vessel. It also works for familiars that do not exist in a physical form.

DIRECTIONS

1. Go into your sacred space.
2. Cast a circle.
3. Intone the following:

> *The circle has been cast*
> *I call upon your power vast*
> *Within the boundaries I have set*
> *Working with no threat*
> *Magickal familiar of mine*
> *I ask that you join me at this time*
> *As I will, so mote it be.*

4. Complete whatever the spell working is.
5. Thank your familiar for their assistance.
6. Open the circle.

TIP ⧉ Cat treats, catnip, and, of course, tuna or salmon are always wonderful offerings for a hardworking feline familiar.

NOTES	SUNDAY	MONDAY	TUESDAY

TIGERS

The tiger is the largest of the big cats. A tiger's energy is a powerful force of strength, control, and determination. Because tigers love water, they also emanate this fluid energy, bringing in strong emotional support.

The stripes of a tiger are not symmetrical, nor do they follow any sort of pattern. Because of this, a tiger animal guide will teach you that you are beautiful just the way you are and to embrace your uniqueness. The tiger helps guide you to emotional stability through their gentle chuffles—a contentment sound unique to big cats, especially tigers—and enables their charge to effectively communicate these emotions to others. Because they have large territories that they must protect, tigers teach us what it means to be able to set and maintain healthy boundaries.

With a tiger as a familiar, you could very well be blessed with "second sight." Tigers have "false eyes" on the back of their ears, thus giving the illusion that they can see in all directions. They also teach us about divine and universal timing and that things come to us when they are meant to.

Reciting this will invoke the power and energies of the tiger.
Burn one orange candle and one black candle.

Energies: Strength, emotional stability, individuality

Fiery strength of will
Wild warrior of the jungle
Do not wake the sleeping tiger
Light and dark
Balance of shadows
Power and grace.

MONDAY

TUESDAY

WEDNESDAY

THURSDAY

FRIDAY

SATURDAY

SUNDAY

MONDAY

TUESDAY

WEDNESDAY

THURSDAY

FRIDAY

SATURDAY

SUNDAY

It is advised to wait until the cat reaches adulthood before consciously pulling on their magick or asking them to lend it.

MONDAY

TUESDAY

WEDNESDAY

THURSDAY

FRIDAY

SATURDAY

SUNDAY

If a feline is in the room when the circle is being cast, you might feel them adding to the boundaries and protection of the circle.

MONDAY

TUESDAY

WEDNESDAY

THURSDAY

FRIDAY

SATURDAY

SUNDAY

Our familiars teach us to believe in ourselves, our power, our intuition, and our ability to send and receive messages.

Cat Whiskers

It is true that cats have heightened senses regarding sight, hearing, and smell. It is the long whiskers of the feline that gives them a physiological advantage. Cat whiskers are highly sensitive. Whiskers help cats find their way and give them feedback about tight spaces and obstacles, all while picking up on subtle energetic vibrations.

Witches can use shed whiskers to "see in the dark." They show us how to make things fit and see ways around any obstacles. Using shed whiskers for divination spells will add a huge boost. They will increase your sensitivity to energies and vibrations and improve your awareness. They can also be used for locator spells to find items that may be lost.

Cats, as high-vibrational beings, and especially familiars, travel frequently in the astral plane. Because whiskers help cats find their way and give them some level of security and protection, they are great to have on hand if you plan to travel into the astral realm. Cat whiskers are known for preventing nightmares as well.

Whiskers are also known for being good luck charms in many cultures. Like wishing on an eyelash to manifest something, cat whiskers are powerful when it comes to manifestation magick. According to old witchcraft, you should whisper your wish into the whisker, and then burn it in the flame of a gold candle. Cat whiskers can be wonderful talismans for getting out of a fix and to help prevent accidents, so keep shed whiskers in your car.

Cats were beloved by the Egyptian goddess Isis, the goddess of magick, who considered them to be personal mediums for her own power. Because of this, a cat's whiskers are revered as powerful catalysts for magickal workings. They will add power to any spell. Shed whiskers can also help with agility, balance, and shedding old ways.

Ritual to Create a Charm Bag for Astral Travel

If you are planning on traveling into the astral realm or fear that you do so in your sleep, this sachet is an effective protection tool.

YOU WILL NEED

- Dried mugwort
- Dried valerian
- Dried rosemary
- Dried lavender
- Selenite
- Amethyst
- Shed cat whiskers
- Small natural-fiber bag that ties

DIRECTIONS

1. Put the dried herbs, crystals, and shed whiskers into the bag, hold it near your crown chakra, and intone the following:

   Into the astral I wish to go
   Please take me there without woe
   Whiskers guide and protect
   From the way home I will not defect.

2. Place the sachet under your pillow at night when you wish to travel into the astral realm or if you fear that you might travel.

TIP ⟨ Shed fur, claws, teeth, and whiskers also make the purrfect offerings to deities such as Bast, Sekhmet, Freya, and Artemis.

NOTES	SUNDAY	MONDAY	TUESDAY

WEDNESDAY	THURSDAY	FRIDAY	SATURDAY

ASTRAL TRAVEL AND PORTALS

All of the metaphysical, mystical, and magickal properties of the feline make them one of the most powerful familiars you could have. It is also because of these properties that familiar spirits choose to take on the form of a cat. While all cats are magickal and can lend their support, the magickal energy summoned when working with a feline familiar is unsurpassed.

Astral Travel: Cats, while nocturnal by nature, will often nap with or near you while you are sleeping. We are most vulnerable during our nonwaking hours, and cats are aware of this. They choose to be near us during that time to offer protection. Some people are prone to astral travel while asleep. The cat is there as a guard to your physical being and a tether to your spirit that is otherwise occupied in the astral realm. Felines also serve as an anchor to this world while you travel. This also holds true if you are engaged in shamanic journey work. You can ask your cat to act as your timer to bring you back or they can gently call you out of the journey if they feel that you have been gone too long.

Portals: Portals are another hot topic when it comes to our feline friends. Portals are gateways that lead to other realms, realities, or dimensions. These can be opened unknowingly or on purpose. Cats are extremely sensitive when it comes to portals and their energies. Cats, especially those that are familiars, have been known to stand guard to ensure that nothing passes through that means us harm. If you ever notice your feline friend returning to the same location in the home repeatedly to just sit, usually looking at a wall or the ceiling, this could mean that there is a portal there. Ask your cat to help you close it and then burn an herb that helps cleanse the space, such as common garden sage, rosemary, or pine. Please call for backup if you feel this portal is beyond your expertise.

MONDAY

TUESDAY

WEDNESDAY

THURSDAY

FRIDAY

SATURDAY

SUNDAY

MONDAY

TUESDAY

WEDNESDAY

THURSDAY

FRIDAY

SATURDAY

SUNDAY

Like messengers, animal guides can also be in corporeal form or reside only in the astral or Spirit realm.

MONDAY

TUESDAY

WEDNESDAY

THURSDAY

FRIDAY

SATURDAY

SUNDAY

The bond with a feline familiar that exists solely on the astral plane is established through magickal workings.

MONDAY

TUESDAY

WEDNESDAY

THURSDAY

FRIDAY

SATURDAY

SUNDAY

If you suddenly see your cat in a dream, this is the cat traveling into the dream/astral world to assist and guide you back.

MONDAY

TUESDAY

WEDNESDAY

THURSDAY

FRIDAY

SATURDAY

SUNDAY

Place a shed whisker in a charm bag with lavender, chamomile, amethyst, and selenite to promote restful sleep and to keep the bad dreams away.

Open to Messages

R emember that your feline familiar will also act as a messenger and a guide for you. If you perform the spell to call them to you, and you are now suddenly dreaming of a cat in a specific location, this is more than likely your familiar communicating with you. They are sending the message of how to find them.

Once you have finally found your way to one another, you can immediately start bonding with your familiar. One way is by talking with them. Remember that this lets them know that you are open to communicating with them. Don't be surprised if you pick up your little ball of fur only to get an image of a can of tuna. They are testing how best to communicate with you and deliver messages. Sometimes it will be through images and sometimes it may come as words in your mind.

They might also lead you directly to something. For instance, you cannot find the incense you want to use for a ritual, and you find yourself asking out loud where it could be. Your cat suddenly jumps up onto the bookcase and is pawing at the back edge. When you pull the bookcase out slightly, you realize that the incense box fell behind there. *Voilà!* Your familiar has led you directly to what you need.

Once you have created this bond with your feline familiar, you will notice that you suddenly seem more plugged into the world of Spirit than ever. Messages come through more clearly and more frequently. Your dreams may be more vivid, and you may recall them more easily. This is what it means to have a cat familiar: they are facilitating communication between the higher realms of Spirit and you. They act as the go-between. Remember that cats are naturally attuned to these energies and when your familiar comes in feline form, this attunement is even greater.

Ritual to Call Your Feline Familiar to You

Use this ritual to call your familiar to you. Be advised that this working must come after you have performed the Ritual to Reveal Your Feline Familiar to You (see 4th month in planner) for it to be of benefit to you.

YOU WILL NEED

- Cat candle or generic cat figurine/photo
- Lighter or matches (if needed)
- A timer (you can use your phone)

TIP ⟨ Once again, if you can find a cat candle, it is recommended for this working. If not, a generic cat figurine or photo will work as well. It is important not to have anything too distinct because you may not know exactly what the cat looks like yet. Aim for silhouettes of cats instead of a photo of a tabby.

DIRECTIONS

1. Go into your sacred space.
2. Place the candle or cat figurine/photo on your altar.
3. Cast a circle.
4. Focus on the energy you felt when you performed the Ritual to Reveal Your Feline Familiar to You.
5. Light the candle if using it or hold the figurine/photo. (**Note**: Be careful when working with fire, taking the necessary precautions.)
6. Intone the following three times:

To my familiar I wish to bond
I call you from the beyond
Being of Spirit and being of power
Come to me in the right and ready hour
The feline form you take
Bringing magick in your wake.
As I will, so mote it be (after the third time).

7. Set the timer for nine minutes and let the candle burn, then snuff it out (or simply hold the figurine/photo for that amount of time).
8. Open the circle. (**Note**: Make sure all fire is out.)

SUNDAY	MONDAY	TUESDAY

WEDNESDAY	THURSDAY	FRIDAY	SATURDAY

MOUNTAIN LIONS

Mountain lions are known to be one with Mother Earth and act as guardians of the mountains. As messengers, they come to us when we need to be shown how to find our balance. They also appear to tell us that we should not be afraid of reaching for something higher.

Anticipate reminders of "look before you leap," to take a breath and come back to center before making a next move. They teach us the meaning of contentment and how to find enjoyment and satisfaction in life. They also show us how to be fierce when needed.

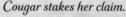

Reciting this will invoke the power and energies of the mountain lion. Burn one tan or light brown candle.

Energies: Balance, adaptability, independence

Perched upon the craggy ledge
Her watchful golden eyes
Patience in the sacred hours
Dawn and dusk
The huntress awaits
Primal and feminine
Power and grace
Sensual and fierce
A perfect balance
Of body, mind, and spirit
Cougar stakes her claim.

MONDAY

TUESDAY

WEDNESDAY

THURSDAY

FRIDAY

SATURDAY

SUNDAY

MONDAY

TUESDAY

WEDNESDAY

THURSDAY

FRIDAY

_____

SATURDAY

_____

SUNDAY

_____

The Hopi, a native Indigenous tribe of North America, believed that the mountain lion was a fierce guardian of their people.

MONDAY

TUESDAY

WEDNESDAY

THURSDAY

FRIDAY

SATURDAY

SUNDAY

Mountain lions, cougars, and pumas bring the same type of energy and powers to their chosen witch.

MONDAY

TUESDAY

WEDNESDAY

THURSDAY

FRIDAY

SATURDAY

SUNDAY

If you are still waiting for your cat familiar, remember that everything comes in the time that it is meant to.

Meditation Work to Seek Spiritual Growth

When we involve our cats in meditation, we find unique advantages to having them near. For starters, they have an immediate calming effect on us. You might notice that the color of the cat factors in during meditation as well, bringing those characteristics to the forefront so that you receive the messages aligned with them. Your feline familiar will sit with you, ensuring that the messages that need to be delivered come through and that you are receiving them in a way that you can understand. Your cat will take you wherever you need to go and bring you back safely.

When going into a meditation, it is important to be able to be still and quiet. You will need to be in a comfortable place that allows for this. Make sure you're not hungry, thirsty, or need to go to the restroom. Closing your eyes helps so that you can relax your body and your mind. Calm your breathing (usually three to six deep breaths in and out) and clear your mind. If any errant thoughts intrude, simply let them float away so that the messages from your higher self, familiar, guides, angels, Deity, or the Universe can come through. Use the following meditation to find what your soul needs for spiritual growth.

YOU WILL NEED

- Purple candle
- Cauldron or fireproof dish
- 1 teaspoon dried mugwort
- Lighter
- 1 tablespoon clear alcohol to help herbs burn (Everclear burns cleanest without extra smoke or smell)
- A timer (you can use your phone)
- Journal and pen

DIRECTIONS

1. Place the candle, cauldron, and mugwort on your altar or in your sacred space and take a seat.
2. Cast a circle.
3. Light the purple candle. (**Note**: Be careful when working with fire, taking the necessary precautions.)
4. Pour the alcohol into the cauldron.
5. Sprinkle in the mugwort, light it with the lighter, and let it burn. (**Note**: Be careful when working with fire, taking the necessary precautions.)
6. Intone the following:

> *Cat medicine for spiritual growth*
> *Guide me and give your oath*
> *To show me what I must address*
> *Help to gain knowledge without duress*
> *Let me see what my soul is seeking*
> *I pledge to listen while you are speaking.*

7. Set the timer for ten to fifteen minutes.
8. Close your eyes and begin the meditation.
9. Once the timer goes off, ground and center yourself.
10. Write down any messages you received, particularly regarding what needs to be done for your soul growth.
11. Open the circle. (**Note**: Make sure all fire is out.)

NOTES	SUNDAY	MONDAY	TUESDAY

WEDNESDAY	THURSDAY	FRIDAY	SATURDAY

MAGICKAL HERBS

All plants have unique vibrational patterns and properties. Here are the basic herbs that can be used alongside your familiar's power to strengthen spells as well as bring your magickal workings to the next level.

Healing: Angelica, yarrow, echinacea, lemon balm, tansy, rosemary, horehound

Protection: Sage, rosemary, pine, juniper, cedar, garlic, rue, nettles, angelica

Communication: Clary sage, rosemary, bay leaf

Love: Red (romance) and pink (self and friends) roses, lavender, vanilla, basil, jasmine

Money: Basil, cinnamon, bay leaf, mint, juniper, cinquefoil, alfalfa

Divination: Mugwort, rosemary, clary sage, dandelion, star anise

Calming/sleep: Lavender, chamomile, lemon balm, bergamot, St. John's wort

Fertility: Pine and spruce (to balance masculine and feminine), cinnamon, nettles, vanilla, willow, red and orange rose petals (to activate root and sacral chakras/sex organs)

Happiness and joy: Marjoram, lavender, St. John's wort, mint, lemon balm, pine

Divine Feminine: Spruce, willow, motherwort, jasmine, mugwort, apple

Divine Masculine: Pine, sunflower, mint, bay leaf, basil, St. John's wort, oak leaves

MONDAY

....

TUESDAY

....

WEDNESDAY

....

THURSDAY

....

FRIDAY

....

SATURDAY

....

SUNDAY

....

MONDAY

TUESDAY

WEDNESDAY

THURSDAY

FRIDAY

SATURDAY

SUNDAY

Cats are as comfortable in the shadows
as they are napping in the sunshine.

MONDAY

TUESDAY

WEDNESDAY

THURSDAY

FRIDAY

SATURDAY

SUNDAY

If you do not have a pet cat, never fear because you still might have a feline as a guide.

MONDAY

TUESDAY

WEDNESDAY

THURSDAY

FRIDAY

SATURDAY

SUNDAY

*Don't be surprised if meditating with a cat
ends up with a journey, be it into a past life
or to another realm.*

MONDAY

TUESDAY

WEDNESDAY

THURSDAY

FRIDAY

SATURDAY

SUNDAY

*Those meditating with cats reported a clear mind
and reaching the alpha state more quickly.*

Cat Claws

As a cat's claws grow, they shed the outer sheath. This is perfectly natural and means that their claws are healthy. You can collect the shed claw sheaths for magickal purposes. The first thing that may come to mind regarding a cat's claws is that they are for defense, and that would be accurate. Shed claws are perfect for protection spells. They can be added to spell jars, sachets, or even lockets that serve as an amulet or talisman. You can even include shed claws in home protection mojo bags, grind them into a powder with other protective herbs, or just sprinkle them around the outside of the home.

If a witch needs to go on the offensive and fight, such as to break hexes and curses, claws are an excellent choice for this, as a cat will use them to attack if necessary. Include them in any working to effectively sever the bindings of a hex or curse. Cat claws used at the time of a Full or Waning Moon along with other cleansing herbs will add a powerful punch to spells or rituals for cutting away what is no longer serving you.

A feline also uses their claws to give them better traction, especially when they initially push off and as they gain momentum at higher speeds during a chase. Use shed claws in spell work to give you a jump start, help with traction, or gain momentum. Having trouble getting into your new workout plan? Maybe a little spell using shed claws will give you that "push off" you need, along with helping to keep your stride once you get going.

Ritual to Create a Spell Jar for Protection

Use this spell jar to keep cat claws near and create a portable protection spell. This spell jar can be left on the altar or taken wherever it is needed, such as in the car or to work.

YOU WILL NEED

- Black candle
- Lighter or matches
- Pen and small piece of paper
- 2 or 3 shed cat claws
- Black obsidian
- Smoky quartz
- Dried sage
- Dried rosemary
- Cleansed small jar with lid or glass vial with stopper

DIRECTIONS

1. Go into your sacred space.
2. Cast a circle.
3. Light the black candle. (**Note**: Be careful when working with fire, taking the necessary precautions.)
4. Write out exactly what the protection spell is for on the piece of paper.
5. Place the cat claws, crystals, and herbs into the jar and chant the following:

> *From my guardian*
> *Claws to defend*
> *Protect and keep safe*
> *Herbs and stones lend their aid*
> *Wax to seal the spell in place*
> *(Drizzle black candle wax to seal the stopper).*
> *So mote it be!*

6. Open the circle. (**Note**: Make sure all fire is out.)

NOTES	SUNDAY	MONDAY	TUESDAY

WEDNESDAY	THURSDAY	FRIDAY	SATURDAY

SPELL FOR PROTECTION

When you are seeking protection through magick, there is an abundance of methods in which you can obtain it. One of the energies of the big cats, the lion, is protection. Cats, by nature, protect us in our most vulnerable hours by staying nearby. Even when we are working within a protected magick circle, if a feline is in the room, they are adding an extra layer of protection for you.

Working magick on a Tuesday or Saturday, during a Full Moon or at noontime, using a black or brown candle, or using black fur, select herbs, and crystals all lend witches protection in their work and life—past, present, and future.

Whichever method you choose to use for protection, do this spell for a little extra boost. All you need is a black candle.

Familiar, guardian, lend me your power
Protection is needed in this hour
Our defenses we will raise
Up around us the barrier stays
Safe with my feline protector
Until it is needed no more.
As I will, so mote it be.

MONDAY

TUESDAY

WEDNESDAY

THURSDAY

FRIDAY

SATURDAY

SUNDAY

MONDAY

TUESDAY

WEDNESDAY

THURSDAY

FRIDAY

SATURDAY

SUNDAY

Cats are simply little magickal fur balls that rule our hearts.

MONDAY

TUESDAY

WEDNESDAY

THURSDAY

FRIDAY

SATURDAY

SUNDAY

The myth of a black cat's bad luck stems from the belief that black cats are haunted because they carry the souls of the departed to hell.

MONDAY

TUESDAY

WEDNESDAY

THURSDAY

FRIDAY

SATURDAY

SUNDAY

Oftentimes, a cat showing up is a reflection of what we need in our life, such as independence and the freedom to be ourselves.

Psychic Bond

Checking in frequently with your feline familiar in regard to the energy of the home and about magickal things in general will help you further strengthen the bond between you. Remember, it is through this bond that they are connecting with you and delivering messages as well as lending power and magick. The stronger the bond, the more easily and effectively the two of you will be able to communicate.

This bond, between familiar and witch, when it is particularly strong creates a psychic link that can be stretched for miles. The benefit of this is that you can both send and receive messages at a distance, and your familiar can lend power and guidance if you need it.

There are stories of psychic links warning the witch or even giving aid from a long distance. This link is important and can be strengthened over time and by working with your familiar. With each message they deliver that you successfully interpret, each spell worked together, and even the evening cuddles, your bond grows and becomes more powerful.

❧ Spell to Anchor for Astral Travel ❧

Use this spell to anchor yourself in the physical realm while traveling in the astral plane. Use a purple candle.

An anchor I will need
Feline familiar stay with me
Keep me safe while I travel
And bring my spirit back from the astral.
So mote it be.

Ritual to Strengthen the Bond with Your Familiar

Use this ritual to strengthen the bond between yourself and your familiar.

YOU WILL NEED

- A purple candle
- Lighter or matches
- Your feline familiar in the room with you

DIRECTIONS

1. Go into your sacred space.
2. Place the candle on your altar.
3. Cast a circle.
4. Light the candle. (**Note**: Be careful when working with fire, taking the necessary precautions.)
5. Hold your cat close if they will let you and intone the following three times:

   The link between familiar and witch
   Closer and stronger we do stitch
   Messages and images we need to share
   We seek now to be more aware
   Through our beings it will lace
   As the psychic bond snaps in place.
   As I will, so mote it be (after the third time).

6. Let the candle burn out.
7. Open the circle. (**Note**: Make sure all fire is out.)

WEDNESDAY	THURSDAY	FRIDAY	SATURDAY

CHEETAHS

The cheetah is the fastest land mammal, reaching speeds of 75 miles per hour (121 km/h), and is all about fast action and quick decisions. But they are also a reminder that we must pace ourselves.

With the cheetah by your side as a guide, they will teach you not only the art of trusting your instincts, but also how vital it can be to act quickly in certain situations. A cheetah's spine is the most flexible of the cats and gives them a biological advantage to increase their speed. This adaption teaches us the importance of remaining flexible in our own lives, giving us an advantage over rigid thinking and closed-mindedness.

As a familiar, the cheetah will help their witch learn how to properly use their own energy and magick. They will remind you that sometimes swift and easy is better than something long and drawn out.

Reciting this will invoke the power and energies of the cheetah.
Burn one yellow candle and one black candle.

Energies: Inner trust, quick action, flexibility

Chasing dreams at the speed of light
It's time to move, go now
Across the savannah
The cheetah's powerful stride
Never missing an opportunity
Trusting in her decisions.

MONDAY

....

TUESDAY

....

WEDNESDAY

....

THURSDAY

....

FRIDAY

....

SATURDAY

....

SUNDAY

....

MONDAY

TUESDAY

WEDNESDAY

THURSDAY

FRIDAY

SATURDAY

SUNDAY

Whether they come as a messenger, guide, or familiar, big cats are to be treasured and revered. Remember that we do not choose them, they choose us.

MONDAY

TUESDAY

WEDNESDAY

THURSDAY

FRIDAY

SATURDAY

SUNDAY

All the cats, big and small, wild cats too, have varying energies and can share different aspects of magick with you.

MONDAY

TUESDAY

WEDNESDAY

THURSDAY

FRIDAY

SATURDAY

SUNDAY

Cats belong to the metaphysical and astral realms and even realms that we humans have not yet ventured into.

Animal Guides

Cats as animal guides are powerful allies, especially for witches, who are able to recognize the significance of having one in their life. They can lend magick and support, help heal, and, of course, guide and teach. Our cat guides remind us to have a spirit of adventure and the curiosity and courage to explore the unknown or subconscious. A feline guide will help you create healthy boundaries and be independent and self-sufficient.

They teach what it means to live in balance with social time and personal time. Cat guides remind us that we can search out our inner truths and connect with our mystical selves without sacrificing the connections within our natural environment. They help us realize that it is not only okay to embrace our wilder nature and the need for freedom, but also that it is imperative to our overall health and wellness.

How do you recognize an animal guide? An animal guide is often an animal that you feel deeply connected to; sometimes it is your favorite animal. Maybe you see a deer every time you are out hiking. Do you often dream of a particular animal? If you notice these things about an animal, wild or domestic, chances are that they are a guide for you.

So how do you know whether a cat is your animal guide? Simply put, you will feel it and the cat will show you. If you have multiple cats, there may be one that you are closer to. Or maybe you have a dog and a cat, and while you love your dog, the bond you share with your cat feels different, deeper. While some might say that cats only serve themselves and have us serve them, the cats that show up as guides in our lives are here to assist us on our journey, so let them. Be still, be open, and listen.

Ritual Recording to Reveal Your Feline Guide to You

Use this ritual to journey to the Lower World and take time to write down your experience in your journal—any messages that come through or special guidance they offer you. Remember that you can make this journey any time you wish to.

1. Close your eyes and take three deep breaths, slowly inhaling and exhaling each one.
2. Imagine yourself in a large meadow. See the grasses moving in the breeze. You notice that there is a forest at the edge of the meadow. You begin to make your way to the trees and you see a path. Follow it. The path through the trees begins to descend a little until you reach a dead end at a massive tree that reaches out in all directions.
3. You notice a large opening at the base of the tree and that the path continues into this opening. This is the entrance to the Lower World and there is a being that guards it.
4. You ask their permission to enter. They allow you access and point to the path that continues onward.
5. The path descends, down, down, down. It winds and spirals down into the Earth until you reach an underground stream.
6. You instinctively lie down in the water and let it wash over you, cleansing you.
7. You step out again on the other side and are dry.
8. You continue on the path until you see an opening with light spilling in. When you reach the opening, you find yourself in a beautiful world with meadows, flowers, trees, and animals of all kinds.
9. There is a bench waiting for you, so you take a seat. In the distance, you can see a feline approaching you. It is your guide and it is time to bond with them.
10. You will stay here until you hear the timer calling you back. When you hear its call, travel back the way you came.

WEDNESDAY	THURSDAY	FRIDAY	SATURDAY

CANDLE MAGICK

Candles are commonplace materials when it comes to rituals and spell work. To reiterate, we incorporate tools such as candle color correspondences because it takes less energy from ourselves and our familiar to work the spell.

Use the following candle correspondences to manifest your magickal intentions.

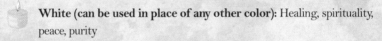 **White (can be used in place of any other color):** Healing, spirituality, peace, purity

Black: Protection, banishing, binding, repelling negative energies, magick (also associated with witches)

Brown: Earth energy (grounding), animals, stability, home protection, family

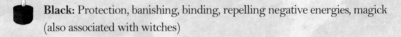 **Red:** Vitality, passion, romantic love, strength, fast action, courage, root chakra

Pink: Self-love, friendship, emotional healing, nurturing

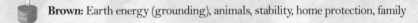 **Yellow:** Happiness, joy, success, power, Sun energy, solar plexus chakra

Orange: Creativity, expression, adventure, positivity, sacral chakra

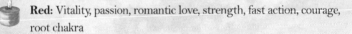 **Green:** Nature, physical healing, money (abundance and prosperity), growth, heart chakra

Blue: Communication, inspiration, calming, throat (royal blue) and third eye (indigo) chakras

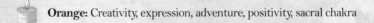 **Purple:** Psychic abilities, hidden knowledge, divination, astral projection, crown chakra

Silver: Divine Feminine, intuition, dreams, Moon energies

Gold: Divine Masculine, wealth, luck, happiness, Sun energies

MONDAY

....

TUESDAY

....

WEDNESDAY

....

THURSDAY

....

FRIDAY

....

SATURDAY

....

SUNDAY

....

MONDAY

TUESDAY

WEDNESDAY

THURSDAY

FRIDAY

SATURDAY

SUNDAY

Our feline familiar's energy naturally syncs with the Moon.

MONDAY

TUESDAY

WEDNESDAY

THURSDAY

FRIDAY

SATURDAY

SUNDAY

*Animal guides and familiars that exist only
in the metaphysical realm can also make
appearances in the physical world.*

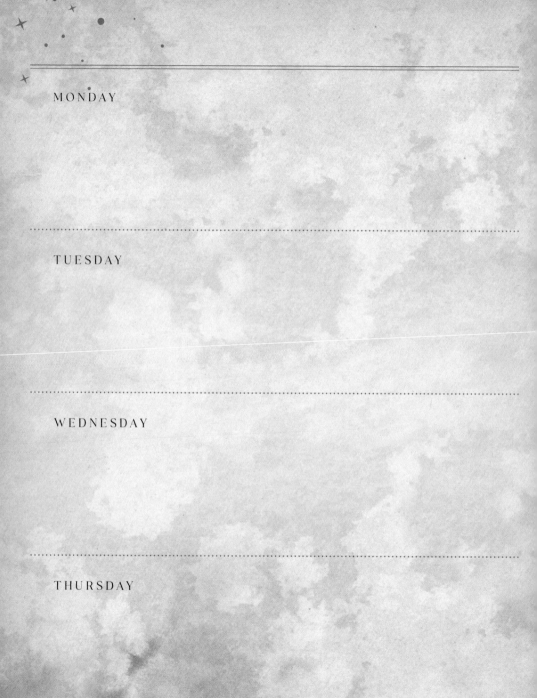

MONDAY

TUESDAY

WEDNESDAY

THURSDAY

FRIDAY

....

SATURDAY

....

SUNDAY

....

As an animal guide, snow leopards will teach you the art of elusiveness and being able to hide in plain sight when necessary.

MONDAY

TUESDAY

WEDNESDAY

THURSDAY

FRIDAY

SATURDAY

SUNDAY

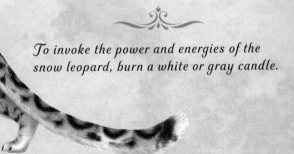

To invoke the power and energies of the snow leopard, burn a white or gray candle.

Ritual for Healing with Cat Medicine

Use this ritual to invoke cat medicine for healing.

- White cat candle (a regular white candle will do, as white is the color of healing)
- Cauldron or fireproof dish
- 1 or 2 small pieces of paper and a pen
- Lighter or matches

DIRECTIONS

1. Find a comfortable place to sit where you will not be disturbed, such as your sacred space.
2. Set the white cat candle and the cauldron on your altar.
3. Cast a circle.
4. Write on a strip of paper what needs to be healed (keep to one or two things at a time so as not to be overwhelmed).
5. Light your candle. (**Note**: Be careful when working with fire, taking the necessary precautions.)
6. Intone the following once:

> *Feline medicine I call to you*
> *We have this work to do*
> *Healing energy is what I need*
> *Bring to me with gentle speed*
> *Whether mind, body, or spirit*
> *Cat medicine come here to heal it.*
> *So mote it be (after the third time).*

7. Say out loud what is written on the paper.
8. Light the paper and drop it into the cauldron.
9. Say the chant twice more (for a total of three times).
10. If any cat in particular showed up for you, thank them for their assistance.
11. Make sure the paper burns completely. As always, be careful when working with open flames.
12. Open the circle. (**Note**: Make sure all fire is out.)
13. Dispose of the spell ash off of your property to ensure that what was plaguing you is not lingering in your space.

NOTE ⸻ Do not trespass on private property to dispose of spell remains. Burying the ash is the preferred method, as the Earth's energy can easily absorb this and transmute it. If this is not possible, it is acceptable to place the spell remains in a garbage receptacle.

NOTES	SUNDAY	MONDAY	TUESDAY

WEDNESDAY	THURSDAY	FRIDAY	SATURDAY

THE HEALING POWER OF THE HOUSE CAT

Our little balls of fur have plenty of medicine to offer all on their own. They are the ultimate Zen masters. They live utterly in the moment, eating when they're hungry, sleeping when they're tired, and playing whenever the urge arises.

Cats know when their human needs healing. How often have you had a rough day at work and once you're home, your cat is winding around your leg and acting extra needy? They are acknowledging that they feel your stress. This simple touch is the cat sharing their auric field with you. Once you sit down and try to relax, they climb onto your chest and start to purr. They are now sharing the stress-relieving and healing vibration that a cat's purr holds.

Anti-anxiety Cat Healing

The cat's purr is a natural anti-anxiety pill. But wait, there's more. The simple act of petting a cat releases oxytocin, which is the "feel good" hormone, reducing stress and anxiety. Some people find that their breathing patterns change while sitting with a cat. They can become subconsciously synchronized and bring on a state of meditative coherence. This in and of itself is mindfulness, compassion, kindness, and love that all come from the heart.

Our feline friends are highly attuned to geopathic energies, the flow of vibrational patterns and disruptions from the Earth. Cats act as buffers for these areas to transmute the unhealthy energy or to break it up altogether. Even while we are unaware, our cats are looking out for us.

MONDAY

TUESDAY

WEDNESDAY

THURSDAY

FRIDAY

SATURDAY

SUNDAY

MONDAY

TUESDAY

WEDNESDAY

THURSDAY

FRIDAY

SATURDAY

SUNDAY

The lunar ties of the majority of felines may bring up strong emotional aspects when calling upon them during a ritual.

MONDAY

TUESDAY

WEDNESDAY

THURSDAY

FRIDAY

SATURDAY

SUNDAY

Be aware that sometimes cat medicine is not as gentle as we would like it to be.

MONDAY

TUESDAY

WEDNESDAY

THURSDAY

FRIDAY

SATURDAY

SUNDAY

The energy from cat medicine will stay with you as long as you need it for continued healing.

MONDAY

TUESDAY

WEDNESDAY

THURSDAY

NOTES

NOTES

NOTES

NOTES

NOTES

NOTES

NOTES

First published in 2024 by Rock Point,
an imprint of The Quarto Group,
142 West 36th Street, 4th Floor
New York, NY 10018, USA
(212) 779-4972
www.Quarto.com

Contains content previously published in 2023 as *Cat Magick* by Rock Point,
an imprint of The Quarto Group, 142 West 36th Street, 4th Floor, New York, NY 10018, USA.

Rock Point titles are also available at discount for retail, wholesale, promotional, and bulk purchase. For details, contact the Special Sales Manager by email at specialsales@quarto.com or by mail at The Quarto Group, Attn: Special Sales Manager, 100 Cummings Center Suite 265D, Beverly, MA 01915 USA.

10 9 8 7 6 5 4 3 2 1

ISBN: 978-1-57715-417-4

Group Publisher: Rage Kindelsperger
Editorial Director: Erin Canning
Creative Director: Laura Drew
Managing Editor: Cara Donaldson
Editor: Katelynn Abraham
Cover Design: Marisa Kwek
Interior Layout: Lorraine Rath
Art by Maggie Vandewalle on the following pages: 1, 5, 20, 67, 119, 169, 221

Printed in China

This planner provides general information on various widely known and widely accepted self-care practices. However, it should not be relied upon as recommending or promoting any specific diagnosis or method of treatment for a particular condition, and it is not intended as a substitute for medical advice or for direct diagnosis and treatment of a medical condition by a qualified physician. Readers who have questions about a particular condition, possible treatments for that condition, or possible reactions from the condition or its treatment should consult a physician or other qualified healthcare professional.